*Poetically Speaking:
Poems for the
Elementary Classroom*

By Georgette G. Lee

Copyright © 2007 Georgette G. Lee
All rights reserved.

ISBN: 1-4196-7186-3
ISBN-13: 978-1419671869

Visit www.booksurge.com to order additional copies.

Dedication

For my husband, Charles, who encourages me;
my teachers who taught me the language and beauty of poetry,
and my students and friends who inspire me.

Table of Contents

Introduction

Part One- Poems About and For School 1
I Am a Teacher 2
The Principal 3
Jess Was In Special Ed. 4
No Child Left Behind? 6
Reading a Book 8
Teacher's Pet 9
Field Trips 10
Clean-Out-Desks Friday 11
Things To Do When I Am Done 12
While I Wait 13
The Seasons 14
Nature's Beauty 15
Fifth Grade Sub 16

Part Two- Fun Poems- Riddles, Nursery Rhymes, Haikus, Name/Acrostic Poems 17
A Riddle… A Riddle… 18
Modern Nursery Rhymes 21
Little Jack Horner 21
Jack and Jill 21, 22
Little Boy Blue 22
Little Miss Muffet 23
Humpty Dumpty 23
Diddle Diddle Dumpling 24
Hey Diddle Diddle 25
Name/Acrostic Poems 26
Georgette 26, 27
Charles 27
Mother 28
Haiku Poems 29

Part Three- Gender Poems 31
Best Friends (females) 32
Best Friends (males) 33
What Are Little Girls Made Of? 34
What Are Little Boys Made Of? 35
Mother 36
Father 37

Part Four- Sensory/ Emotional Poems 39
Happiness 40
Anger 42
Disappointment 43
Sensory Poems- At School 44
At the Park 45
At the Mall 46
At the Beach 47

Part Five- Figurative Language 49
A Simile Rap 50
Color Metaphors 52
Synonym Walk 54
An Antonym Poem 57
Prefixed Antonyms 59
Symbols 60
Number Symbolism 62
Alliteration 63
Idioms: It's Raining 65
Onomatopoeia 67
Surround Sounds 68
Personification 69

Part Six- Template Poems 71
I Have 72
Yesterday 75
I Know Who I Am 77
About the Author 79

Introduction

To the Teacher:

Teaching Poetry can be so much fun, yet many teachers steer away from the genre of poetry. The purpose of this collection of poems is to equip teachers with a variety of poems and activities that introduce students to reading, writing, and enjoying poetry. The book is divided into six major sections. Part one has poems related to school with which the students can readily identify. Part two offers fun poems like riddles and nursery rhymes, haiku, and name/acrostic poems. Students can have fun creating these idiosyncratic poems.

Part three features gender poems. These poems can be used to explore differences and similarities of the sexes in terms of activities they enjoy, personalities, and the dynamics of their friendships and relationships. Part four features sensory and emotional poems. Students can explore emotions and increase their sensitivity to life through reading and writing these kinds of poems. Part five is called figurative language. The idea behind this segment is to help teachers introduce students to an important element of literature. These poems can be used to reinforce the various strands of figurative language as they emerge in the literature unit. They can be used to help promote literary understanding and to assist students in later pursuing themes and underlying meanings as they step into the world of analyzing poems.

The final section, part six is called template poems. I coined this term since the poem is used as a template to generate similar poems. Just like one would trace a picture, the students follow either the beginning or ending of a line of a poem to write their own poem. Students remove the base or the stem of a line and add their personal phrase. The integrity of the poem is maintained, while creating a new poem.

Teaching and learning about poetry should be fun for the teacher and the student alike. *Poetically Speaking* seeks to demonstrate that poetry is a genre in which all can successfully engage. After all, poetry is a form of self expression, and each of us has something to express. Let us have fun as we speak poetically, not only in the classroom, but also in our everyday conversations.

Tips for Teachers for a Sane School Year...

Tell your students how much you appreciate them.

Exercise your mind- think of the many creative ways you can teach the same subject.

Ask tons of questions-better safe than sorry.

Carry away some knowledge from the students each day.

Help the students find their way.

Erase painful experiences by starting each day with an expectation of hope.

Reduce stress factors: take deep breaths before responding to frustrating situations.

Speak poetically.

To the Student:

Every year, my students and I engage in a poetry unit where we select, read, and dramatize a variety of poems. My students also write their own poems. They understand that poems do not have to rhyme, although they do have a special beat or rhythm that separates them from other forms of writing. As you go through the different parts of this book, you will have fun learning about and creating the varied types of poems introduced here.

In part one, you will be able to identify with the poems about school and other related themes. You can write your own riddles, nursery-rhymes, Haikus and name/acrostic poems similar to those found in section two, and the gender poems of section three. Part four offers an arena for venting your emotions and using your senses as you read and write sensory/emotional poems.

Part five features an array of figurative elements with which you will come into contact in your English/Language Arts class. This section serves as a handy reference to those literary elements which sometimes seem difficult to grasp. The poems exemplify selected figurative devices and make them easy to understand.

In part six, you will read about template poems and easily write new poems by 'tracing' the original template poem given.

Poetry need not be a drab subject. Actually, it is a form of self expression. Since we all have something to say, why not say it with flair. I invite you to speak poetically as you go through the poems in this collection. Have fun!

Tips for students for a sane school year...

Study hard.

Talk with your teachers: Ask for explanations when in doubt.

Utilize your time wisely.

Devote a daily time period for study and homework.

Exercise your mind- learn something new each day.

Never put off for tomorrow what can be done today.

Tell your teachers how much you appreciate them.

Speak poetically.

PART ONE

POEMS ABOUT AND FOR SCHOOL

POETICALLY SPEAKING

I Am a Teacher

I am a teacher

Who stands tall and proud

To fill minds every day,

I have a huge responsibility,

It matters what I say.

I open doors of destiny

To kids who sit in front of me,

They learn from my actions too,

It matters what I do.

I can make them with a positive word

Or break them with a scorn,

A child's future depends on me-

In my class genius is born.

I am a teacher

Who stands tall and proud

To ignite a vital spark, I teach academics and give value

To open minds and eager hearts,

And I impact the crowd.

I am a teacher

Who stands tall and proud.

POEMS ABOUT AND FOR SCHOOL

The Principal

She enters happily our classroom,

"Good Morning, students, how are you?"

"Great!" the children all agree,

For the principal they are delighted to see.

She takes a good look around our space,

And sees that learning we embrace,

We've placed words and numbers on our walls,

"What is this word?" to me she calls,

I talk about a horizontal line.

"Great, you are doing fine."

She knows all of the students' names,

The Davids, the Joans, the Dans, the Janes.

When we read our books in the cafeteria,

She rewards us with a pretty sticker,

I love our principal, she really cares,

And adds joy to our school days.

Jess Was In Special Ed.

Ring, Ring, the school bell sang
It's time to start the day,
Jess entered class without a bang-
Hardly a word to say.
You see, he did not care for school,
He could barely read or write.
Most people thought he was a fool,
So he gave up without a fight.

Jess got his letters and sounds mixed up,
That stuff just wasn't clear.
He felt hopeless inside a book,
School did not make his day.

But that fall while in grade four-
Special Ed. they called his set,
A new teacher entered the door,
Raising the bar for what to expect.
She saw that Jess hardly spoke,
He seemed so shy and sad.
His helplessness the teacher broke
Dared him to be a learner glad.
"All of you can learn," she said aloud,
"But you must try really hard."
"Don't give up, don't be cowed,

For reading should not be a barb."
Every one has a special talent
To help them along life's journey.
That gift when given nourishment
Propels them toward destiny.

Well Jess, he had a marvelous memory
Which in class served him fine,
He could recall where he saw a key term-
The exact book, the page, and the line.

So when he wanted to spell 'dinosaur'
He rushed to the class library
To locate the word for his writing chore,
And to add to his word dictionary.
Pretty soon Jess was more vocal in class,
He was learning to read and spell,
He offered to read out loud at last,
As his confidence began to swell.
Jess moved on to fifth grade a happy lad,
He could do anything, he now believed,
The teacher made learning a joy,
And used Jess' strength to help him achieve.

No Child Left Behind?

I have Grade five ISAT to take,
But I'm reading at grade two,
They place the scripts in front of me,
I don't know what to do.

The teacher reads the instructions,
But that's all she dares do,
I cannot read what's on the sheet,
I haven't got a clue.

Although my reading level has soared
By two grade levels or three,
That's not mirrored in the test scores,
That doesn't seem fair to me.

So when the test results are back,
Below the standards I will score,
Or placed on academic warning,
My confidence will be no more.

I am being left behind
In every kind of way,
Though meeting goals on my IEP,
It is the ISAT that I greatly fear.

They place me on the bottom rung

In a class of inclusion,

While those around me often laugh

At my down right confusion.

'No child left behind', they fuss,

I tried my very best,

What happens when that's not good enough,

And I still don't pass the test?

Reading a Book

I just can't wait to read a book,
To visit places far and near,
It maybe a cute country nook,
Or some striking city with flair.

I search out a new word or phrase
To apply when I speak and write,
And when I'm working with my peers,
That makes me appear rather bright.

I can choose an informative text,
Perhaps a how-to- manual,
Maybe a persuasive pamphlet,
Or possibly a funny journal.

Whenever I get to read the lines
I'm becoming a better me;
Not just passing away the time,
But forming my personality.

I just can't wait to read a book,
It offers so much fun,
Once you get started you are hooked,
From the start until you are done.

Teacher's Pet

You call her 'teacher's pet' as if
She wears a badge of shame,
But to the teacher she's a gift,
And earns her point of fame.

Who brings in homework right on time,
Has the right word to give,
Who in the classroom all outshines,
Whose brain seems not a sieve?

Who volunteers to do a task,
Is there to lend a hand,
Who in the teacher's knowledge bask,
Against the cheaters stand?

Who is the kindest child around,
And such a joy to teach?
She is fixed, focused, duty-bound,
You wish she were for keeps.

You call her teacher's pet as if
It's a shame to be so,
Get a concept definition shift,
Teacher's pet- the way to go.

POETICALLY SPEAKING

Field Trips

Do you enjoy field trips?

I most certainly do!

Sometimes we go to the petting zoo,

Sometimes we go to roller skate,

Or visit the supermarket,

Sometimes we climb aboard a ship,

And around the city we take a trip,

Sometimes we take in a movie or play,

Sometimes we go to a book fair,

Sometimes we go to the museum,

Or visit the sea aquarium.

Going on field trips is so much fun,

But apart from that, we learn a ton!

POEMS ABOUT AND FOR SCHOOL

Clean-Out-Desks Friday

Today's the day we clean our desks,

There're always such a horrible mess,

Pencil-stubs and shavings to throw away,

Keep the spelling sheet since you got an A,

Crunched-up paper to toss in the bin,

We're making clean our surroundings.

If we clean out our desks like the teachers say,

They will be sparkling come Monday!

Things to Do When I Am Done

I can read a short story,

I can write 'All About Me',

I can study a chapter,

I can recheck my paper,

I can help my peer buddy,

I can read some poetry,

I can learn a few new words,

I can identify verbs,

I can practice a new skill,

I can do a number drill,

I can do a word puzzle,

I can learn a times table,

I can do creative writing,

I can do Word-Wall spelling,

Lots to do when I am done,

Learning while still having fun!

POEMS ABOUT AND FOR SCHOOL

While I Wait

Sitting in the big, open café,

School is out and there is not a care.

The music soothes, and the air is light,

I reminisce on summer's delight.

I think about life way back then,

Things we have done and places we've been.

There wasn't money for travels far,

We took the bus, 'cause there was no car.

Most of the time we laughed and we talked,

As we made lively the arduous walk.

We donned our swim suits, strolled down to the beach,

Into the water when there we reached.

Swum, lay-floated and mindlessly played,

Burnt skins and red eyes- the price we paid.

Built sand castles, sea shells collected,

Our hungry bellies we neglected.

At the end of the day, strength almost gone,

Just enough left for the walk back home.

POETICALLY SPEAKING

The Seasons

Buried beneath the barren snow

Are flowers just waiting to grow,

When the rain and sunshine step in

Life greets the wake-up call of spring.

Then sleeping beauties will awake,

Old winter drabness they will shake,

The rays of sun will add its heat,

Nature dances to the spring beat.

School is out and we celebrate

A lengthy fun-filled summer's break,

Camping, fishing, traveling fun,

Darkened skins from the broiling sun.

Watch the green turn to red and brown,

The vast fields wear a golden crown,

Temperatures drop, plants bow their heads,

Nature must hurry back to bed.

Nature's Beauty

No face can have the beauty of
The stars up in the sky,
No book can hold more stories than
The volume of the eye.
No perfume can be more fragrant
Than freshly fallen rain,
No being's strength can exceed
That of any mountain.
No diamond can have the splendor
Of moonlight on the sea,
No musician can outclass
A nightingale's melody.
No gown can be lovelier
Than a blooming flower,
No crime can be a mystery
To match a passing hour.
No money can give enrichment
More than a new born child,
No jewel's sparkle can transcend
That of a radiant smile.
Nature's gifts are highly assessed,
Yet all of them are free,
And none on earth can half compare
With nature's rare beauty.

Fifth Grade Sub

The students got a sub today,

They saw it as a time to play,

The math they said was way too hard,

Their behavior was very bad.

The children claimed they could not read,

The in-class rules they would not heed,

They laughed, they frolicked, and they yelled,

The poor sub was saved by the bell.

By day's end she felt a mess,

She rested her head on the desk,

Her temples gave an aching throb,

God bless the one who does this job.

For the teacher she left a note,

"I applaud you, I could not cope."

"What goes around must come around,

For when in school, I played class clown."

PART TWO

FUN POEMS - RIDDLES, NURSERY RHYMES, HAIKUS, NAME/ACROSTIC POEMS

A Riddle… A Riddle…

I have an eye

But I cannot see,

If your socks have a hole

Then you would need me.

What am I?

(A needle)

I have ears

But I cannot hear,

I'm delicious to eat

Any time of day.

What am I?

(Corn)

I have a tongue

But I cannot speak,

When you're stepping out

Just put me on your feet.

What am I?

(Shoes)

I have three feet

But I cannot walk,

I can tell you a measurement

Although I cannot talk.

What am I?

(A yard stick)

I have a big head

But no mouth or teeth,

I'm leafy and round

And go well with corn beef.

What am I?

(Cabbage)

I have teeth

But I cannot eat,

You need me around

To keep your hair neat.

What am I?

(A comb)

Modern Nursery Rhymes

Little Jack Horner

Little jack Horner

Sat in a corner

On the time-out chair,

He made a mistake,

Didn't know it was fake,

And pulled off Suzie's hair.

Jack and Jill

Jack and Jill went up the hill

To see who ran the faster,

Jill worked up a great pace

To easily win the race,

And poor jack was the loser.

Jack and Jill

Jack and Jill

Ran up the hill

To see who would be faster,

Jack stubbed his toe,

Oh! No! No! No!

But still ended up the winner.

Little Boy Blue

Little Boy Blue

Could not tie his shoe,

And kept falling all over the floor,

Until a trip to the store

Led Mom to Velcro,

And Boy Blue now trips no more.

Little Miss Muffet

Little Miss Muffet

Sat on a tuffet

Eating her low-fat yogurt,

She was on a diet

And wanted to lose weight,

Until she could fit a size eight.

Little Miss Muffet

Little Miss Muffet

Sat on a tuffet,

Eating her cake and ice cream,

Along came a bee

And sat on her knee,

And boy did Miss Muffet SCREAM!

Humpty Dumpty

Humpty Dumpty

Had a great fall

While out for recess,

The school nurse checked him out,

And without a doubt

He went back to play,

Humpty Dumpty was fine

For the rest of the day.

Diddle Diddle Dumpling

Diddle Diddle Dumpling

My son John

Went to bed

With his school clothes on.

He must have had a rough day,

He rushed through the door

Up the stairway,

And sound asleep

In bed he lay.

Hey Diddle, Diddle

The cat scratched dad's fiddle

While chasing a tiny mouse,

Though dad was not happy,

It sure looked funny

Seeing those three-

The cat, mouse and daddy

Running all over the house.

POETICALLY SPEAKING

Name/Acrostic Poems:

Write a name down in a vertical line using capital letters. Then write descriptive words or phrases beginning with each capitalized letter.

GEORGETTE

Gorgeous and glamorous,

Eager to learn and grow,

Open to new ideas,

Respect I strive to show,

Gleeful and joyous,

Excellence is my motto,

Talented and creative,

Tenacious and thorough,

Erudite and imaginative,

A world of love to give.

Giving

Ever,

Often

Relaxing,

Gloriously

Exciting,

Tenderly

Touching,

Embracing humanity!

Charming

Handsome

Affectionate

Reliable

Loyal

Eloquent

Sweet …

That's my husband Charles,

Together we're complete.

M is for the world's best mother,

O is for her sense of order,

T is for her touch so tender

H is for her heavenly chatter,

E is for her earnest eyes,

R is for her radiant smile.

MOTHER

Haiku Poems

Haiku is a short Japanese poem having 17 syllables. There are three unrhymed lines that usually tell about nature. The first and last lines have five syllables each, and the middle line has seven syllables. More contemporary Haiku poems tell about subjects other than nature.

Saturday evening,

Strolling leisurely in the

Park, enjoying peace.

Flowers are blooming,

Birds singing, light rain falling,

Illinois in spring.

The wind howled gruffly,

As a flock of battered leaves

Whirled swiftly past me.

Sitting at my desk,

Attending to the teacher,

Gaining much knowledge.

Hip-moving music,

Tasty meals, meeting friends, a

Taste of Chicago.

Hope has no limits,

Refuses all boundaries,

Knows no restrictions.

Love conquers all doubts,

Negates all opposition,

Sustains all our dreams.

PART THREE

Gender Poems

Best Friends (females)

We chat and laugh for hours,

We ride out to the park,

We pick our favorite flowers,

We say 'bye before dark.

At lunch we eat together,

We share a tasty snack,

We look out for one another,

We have each other's back.

We keep each other's secrets,

And promise not to tell,

We know the other's habits,

We treat each other well.

Best friends we are forever,

A vow made from the heart,

Always there for each other,

True friends who'll never part.

GENDER POEMS

Best Friends (males)

Though friends, we wrestle and fight,

We watch horror movies at night,

We enjoy playing video games,

We call each other out our names.

For weekend fun we go bowling,

In the summer we go camping

And exchange the scariest tales,

We saw hard wood and hammer nails.

We try to catch the biggest fish,

Or throw a huge stone the farthest,

We skin our knees and we don't cry,

The roughest tasks we dare to try.

We know we are the best of friends,

And on each other we depend.

Though it has never been remarked…

We know it deep inside our hearts.

What Are Little Girls Made Of?

What are little girls made of?

Little girls are made of

Hugs and kisses and…

A great bundle of love.

Pink and pastels in their bedrooms,

Stories of princes and fairy tale 'toons,

Ribbons and lace, broad-rimmed hats,

Coloring books, and cell phone chats,

Modeling, mothering, imaginative play,

Giggling, chattering, secrets to share,

Bratz dolls, reading books, and tea sets,

Colliers, kittens and furry pets,

What are little girls made of?

Hugs and kisses and

A great bundle of love.

GENDER POEMS

What Are Little Boys Made Of?

What are little boys made of?

Little boys are made of

Hugs and kisses and…

A great bundle of love.

Blue and bold hues in their bedrooms,

Spider Man, and heroic cartoons,

Jeans and corduroys and durable wear,

Climbing, running, physical play,

Hip hop culture, and clean raps,

Trains, soccer balls, baseball bats,

Computers, comic books, video games,

Skiing, and sledding down the fast lanes,

Lizards, snails, and wiggly worms,

Throw them to sis and make her squirm.

What are little boys made of?

Hugs and kisses and…

A great bundle of love.

POETICALLY SPEAKING

<u>Mother</u>

She steps in to dry my tears,

She's in my corner with the loudest cheers,

She teaches me right from wrong,

She shows me how to stay strong,

She's a friend who lends her ears,

She easily calms all my fears,

She always lends a helping hand,

And on my side she proudly stands,

I will trade her for no other,

She'll always be my dear mother.

Her kiss miraculously heals

My scrapes, cuts, bumps and peels,

She nurses me throughout the night,

And in the morning I'm alright,

With her I 'm never a bother,

She'll always be my dear mother.

GENDER POEMS

Father

He taught me how to ride a bike,

He showed me how to fly a kite,

He takes me on a motor cycle ride

And I feel so good inside,

He puts me high upon his back

Then I'm the tallest of the pack,

He showed me how to pitch a ball,

And how to make a bird call,

We dig the worms to use as bait,

And then we fish out on the lake,

He plays a lot of games with me,

He reads me a bed-time story.

He is incredibly strong,

He tells me when I'm doing wrong,

He is full of joy and laughter,

My dad, my buddy, my dear father.

PART FOUR

SENSORY/EMOTIONAL POEMS

POETICALLY SPEAKING

Exploring Feelings through Poetry:

Take an emotion like **happiness**, and write a number of sentences telling of what makes you happy. Lines do not have to rhyme, but you can rearrange the sentences and use synonyms to make lines rhymes.

HAPPINESS

I am happy when…

The work that I studied

Shows up on the test,

I have a hard exam,

But did my very best.

The results are finally back

And I get an A-

What a terrific feeling

To last throughout the day.

I am happy when…

I get to go shopping

With very little cash,

And I spot a great bargain

With half the price slashed.

SENSORY/EMOTIONAL POEMS

It is the week end and

I get to sleep in late,

Watch my favorite movies,

That's time to celebrate!

I am happy when…

I eat my favorite dish,

I get just what I wish,

A child gets what I teach,

For that's someone I've reached.

I am happy then!

<u>ANGER</u>

I am angry when…

I don't know what to do,

I can't find a matching shoe,

I misplace a special thing

Like a number or a ring,

I get into a big fight,

I just don't get it right,

I do not get my way,

I don't know what to say.

DISAPPOINTMENT

I am disappointed when…

I flunk one of my tests,

One does not keep a promise,

Or fails to do his best,

My team loses the game,

And hang their heads in shame.

I am disappointed when…

It rains on my parade,

The sun blocks out the shade,

People forget my birthday,

It seems they do not care,

I do not get a gift,

Even though I sent a list.

Sensory Poems:

Use the five senses to write about a variety of topics. Begin each line with one of the senses.

<u>At School</u>

I see the children's eager faces,

I hear their questions- so many uncertainties,

I smell the lingering scent of ten sweaty bodies,

I touch the crinkled pages of their note books,

I taste their quest for knowledge.

SENSORY/EMOTIONAL POEMS

At the Park

I see the vibrant-colored flowers,

I hear the happy voices of playing children,

I smell the fresh, moist air by the lake,

I touch the rough rope of the swing.

After biking on the trail,

I taste the beads of sweat streaming down my face,

I feel rather worn and I look a bit pale-

I'm no longer a youngster.

At the Mall

I see the modern fashions in the store windows,

I hear the voices of chatty cell-phone users,

I smell the pop corn and cotton candy,

I'm feeling a bit hungry,

I taste the cheese pizza and pop.

I touch the soft fabric of the dress

With a tender caress,

I have shopped and almost dropped,

It's time to go home and rest.

SENSORY/EMOTIONAL POEMS

At the Beach

I see the sea gulls fight over crumbs,

I hear the waves lash against the shore,

I smell the fresh, moist air,

I feel my cares drift away.

I touch the warm, coarse sand,

I taste the salty ocean spray.

I prop my head against my hand,

It's another glorious day.

PART FIVE

FIGURATIVE LANGUAGE

Figurative Language

Figurative language is a literary device that makes writing more descriptive and interesting. Figurative language calls the reader to look at ordinary things in a new and unusual way.

A **simile** is a comparison made between two unlike things using the words 'like' or 'as'.

A Simile Rap

As pretty as a flower,

As clean as a shower,

As tall as a tower,

As shady as a bower.

As hot as boiling water,

As greasy as butter,

As indistinct as a mutter,

As confusing as clutter.

As dark as a berry,

As red as a cherry,

As wobbly as jelly,

FIGURATIVE LANGUAGE

As round as a swollen belly.

As brown as iron rust,

As light as dust,

As crispy as a crust,

As strong as a wind gust.

As sharp as a knife,

As easy-going as life,

As fast as frightened mice,

As loving as a new wife.

As hungry as a bear,

As heavy as a care,

As happy as a cheer,

As scornful as a jeer.

As cruel as death,

As wearisome as a pest,

As quiet as rest,

As funny as a jest.

Metaphors:

Metaphors (like similes) are comparisons between two unlike things, but the words 'like' or 'as' are not used. You say that one thing is something else. Instead of saying, "I'm as pretty as a flower, you would say, "I'm a pretty flower". Some metaphors are formed with color words.

Color Metaphors

You may be green with envy,

Perhaps bright red with rage,

Blue means you are feeling sad,

If luke-warm, that goes with beige.

Black, darkness and doom bellows,

White stands for purity,

Cowards are called yellow,

Green means you harbor envy.

Red screams, "Beware of danger!"

Blue and gloom walk together,

Brown is humbly down-to-earth,

When grey you are lacking mirth.

FIGURATIVE LANGUAGE

Peach is quite illustrious,

Orange is loud and boisterous,

Gold speaks of strength and much wealth,

Pink says you are in good health.

Lilac says weak and sickly,

Silver means stability,

Purple goes with royalty-

Speaking metaphorically.

Synonyms:

Synonyms are words that have the same, or nearly the same, meaning. The word nice is often overused. Friendly, helpful, attractive, and delightful are synonyms for the word nice.

Synonym Walk

Walk together children,

For you are the same,

Only being called by

A different name.

Young lady, female, lass, girl,

Spiral, curve, curl, swirl,

Fellow, male, lad, boy,

Introverted, timid, shy, coy.

Leap, jerk, dance, jig,

Mammoth, large, huge, big,

Rugged, harsh, course, rough,

Hard, difficult, thick, tough.

Merry, cheery, joyful, happy,

FIGURATIVE LANGUAGE

Exhausted, fatigued, tired, weary,

Forlorn, unhappy, dejected, sad,

Enraged, insane, angry, mad.

Walk together children,

For you are equal,

Indistinguishable,

And interchangeable.

Earnest, powerful, forceful, strong,

Unsuitable, evil, not-right, wrong,

Stainless, spotless, guiltless, clean,

Wiry, skinny, lanky, lean.

Deft, clutter-free, tidy, neat,

Tuneful, delightful, sugary, sweet,

Rancid, bitter, tangy, sour,

Slouch, shrink, crouch, cower.

Poor, destitute, broke, needy,

Rich, affluent, lush, wealthy,

Kind, caring, cordial, mild,

Baby, babe, infant, child.

Walk together children,

For you are alike,

Only being seen

In a different light.

FIGURATIVE LANGUAGE

Antonyms:

Antonyms are words that are opposite in meaning.

An Antonym Poem

Antonyms are opposites,

They do not agree,

When one is Bond,

The other is Free.

When one is Right, the other is Wrong,

When one is Weak, the other is Strong,

When one is Left, the other is Right,

When one is Loose, the other is Tight,

When one is Dull, the other is Bright,

When one is Dark, the other is Light,

When one is Day the other is Night.

Antonyms are opposites,

They have separate lives,

When one Laughs,

The other one Cries.

When one is Rich, the other is Poor,

When one is Fast, the other is Slow,

When one says Yes, the other says No,

When one Admits, the other Denies,

When one Sells, the other one Buys.

When one Goes, the other one Comes.

When one Walks, the other one Runs,

When one Starts, the other is Done,

When one is Boring, the other is Fun.

When one Gives, the other one Gets,

When one is Dry, the other is Wet,

When one is Quiet, the other is Loud,

When one is Ashamed the other is Proud.

Antonyms are opposites,

They just cannot agree,

When one is Enslaved,

The other is Free.

FIGURATIVE LANGUAGE

Some **Antonyms** are formed using prefixes. A prefix is a syllable added to the front of a word to change its meaning.

Prefixed Antonyms

Trust and mistrust, Just and unjust,

Willing and unwilling, Fitting and unfitting,

Skillful and unskillful, Truthful and untruthful,

Manageable and unmanageable, Agreeable and disagreeable,

Honorable and dishonorable, Loyal and disloyal,

Color and discolor, Favor and disfavor,

Adequate and inadequate, Fortunate and unfortunate,

Grateful and ungrateful, Lawful and unlawful,

Kind and unkind, Wind and unwind,

Worthy and unworthy, Steady and unsteady,

Modest and immodest, Interest and disinterest,

Arm and disarm, Harm and unharmed.

Symbols:

Symbols are things that are used to represent something else. For example, the heart is a symbol of love, and a dove is a symbol of peace.

Symbols

A circle represents eternity,

No beginning, no end,

Forever we will be.

A lily is a symbol of purity,

A flower is a symbol of beauty,

Water is a symbol of life,

The sword is a symbol of strife.

Gems represent wealth,

An apple represents good health,

Gold is a symbol of prosperity,

Winter is a symbol of austerity.

FIGURATIVE LANGUAGE

The Bible is a symbol of truth,

Milk is a symbol of youth,

A crown is a symbol of royalty,

A scepter is a symbol of authority.

The symbol of peace is a dove,

The heart is a symbol of love,

A symbol of hope is the rainbow,

A symbol of purity is snow.

A snake symbolizes deception,

A fist symbolizes determination,

A scale is a symbol of justice,

A war medal is a symbol of service.

A circle represents eternity,

No beginning, no end,

Forever we will be.

POETICALLY SPEAKING

Number Symbolism

ONE speaks of unity

and supremacy,

TWO speaks of division

sprung from confusion,

THREE speaks of perfection,

FOUR is the number of earth-

east, west, south, north,

FIVE is the number of grace,

good manners, and charm,

While **SIX** is the number of man,

SEVEN speaks of completion,

EIGHT speaks of new beginnings,

and rejuvenation,

NINE speaks of evaluation,

TEN- well, take away the zero

And you're back to **ONE**,

which is where it all begun.

FIGURATIVE LANGUAGE

Alliteration

Alliteration is the repetition of initial sounds in a word. It creates tongue-twisters. See how quickly you can read this alliterative poem.

Alliteration

Angry Andrew anticipated an antagonizing day.

Bold Betty bolted down the battered bay.

Capable Carl carried the colossal calf.

Daring David dangled dangerously from the raft.

Ellen the eager eagle eased elegantly down the shoot.

Floyd the fly fluttered in the flute.

Gale the gangly girl gazed at the grizzly bear.

Hilarious Harry hollered at the hurried hare.

Impossible Ivy invaded the internet site.

Juggling Judy jumped across the jagged dike.

Lazy Lucy lounged in the luminous lake.

Merry Mary marched as she mended the chipped plate.

POETICALLY SPEAKING

Naughty Nancy nudged the quiet child,

Outlandish Orman lived in the open wild.

Precious Pearl placed the pretty flower in the pot.

Quaint Quincy quivered though it was quite hot.

Rough Roger rolled down the rugged ridge.

Silly Sally stalled on the stony bridge.

Tipsy Turvey turned the twisted tunnel.

Ugly Ulah floated down the funnel.

Victorious Victoria wore the victor's vest.

Wendy was the winner of the wired waist contest.

Xylophone, xenophobia, x-ray,

Yasmin yanked the young girl's hair,

Zena zapped the zagged zipper.

FIGURATIVE LANGUAGE

Idioms:

Idioms are another form of figurative language.

An idiom does not mean exactly what it says. 'Mary found herself in a stew' does not mean that Mary was actually in a pot of stew. It means that Mary was in trouble. See if you know the idioms in this poem.

It's Raining

It's <u>*raining cats and dogs*</u> out there,

So we cannot go out to play,

Why <u>*make a mountain of a molehill*</u>?

There are other things to be done still.

Meanwhile, I could <u>*catch forty winks*</u>,

And I'd be up before mom blinks,

"Have you <u>*lost your mind*</u>?" She might ask,

If she sees my incomplete tasks.

So I should <u>*strike while the iron is hot*</u>,

And start to wash those pans and pots,

Then mother will be <u>*tickled pink*</u>,

When she sees the clean kitchen sink.

Hit the nail full on the head,

Please do not go back to bed.

There's no time left to *drag your feet*,

Play only after work is complete.

If the rain does not go away,

Then we can play another day.

FIGURATIVE LANGUAGE

Onomatopoeia

Onomatopoeia is sounds or words that imitate or sound like the word they refer to...

Onomatopoeia

Boom! Boom! Boom! belched the drum,

Judy slammed shut the door,

The dog gave an angry growl,

As he curled up on the floor.

The sleepy cat purred softly,

Snuggled warmly on the mat,

The fire gave a sharp crackle,

Interrupting my short nap.

An engine sputtered to a start,

Somewhere out in the dark night,

These wintry sounds came to a stop,

A quick hush before day light.

Surround Sounds

"Tick tock!" goes the clock,

"Splash!" goes the water

As the boy dives off the dock.

"Pop!" goes the balloon

With a loud burst in the room.

"Maa, Maa," bawls the baby

Rudely woken from her sleep,

"Clappity-Clap! Clippity-Cleep!"

Sing the slippers on mother's feet.

FIGURATIVE LANGUAGE

Personification:

Personification is treating a lifeless object or thing as a human being, giving it human qualities, or representing it in human form. Death is often personified as a grim reaper. How many examples of personification can you identify in the poem below?

Rain drops dancing on my windowpane,

Spring flowers drink up the falling rain,

Looks like the weeds have gone insane,

They have invaded mother's garden.

The sun has closed her drooping eyes,

Time for the moon to supervise,

As night winds sing their lullabies,

"To bed my child," they sweetly sigh.

PART SIX

TEMPLATE POEMS

I Have

I have traveled to the edge and back…

I have seen cows with bells,

I have walked tirelessly,

I have lived like a gypsy,

I have cried bitterly,

I have laughed at myself,

I have sung melodiously,

I have danced to calypso music,

I have dreamed daringly,

I have pursued happiness,

I have traveled to the edge and back.

TEMPLATE POEMS

I have traveled to Europe and back

I have seen distantly,

I have walked in the snow-capped mountains,

I have lived relentlessly,

I have cried when someone died,

I have laughed uncontrollably,

I have sung "I Believe I Can Fly",

I have danced rhythmically,

I have dreamed that I could fly,

I have pursued life fearlessly.

I have traveled to the edge and back.

POETICALLY SPEAKING

Now write you own "I Have" poem using the template below:

I Have

        I have traveled

        I have seen

        I have walked

        I have lived

        I have cried

        I have laughed

        I have sung

        I have danced

        I have dreamed

        I have pursued

        I have traveled

TEMPLATE POEMS

Yesterday

Yesterday I met a friend,

We exchanged names and

Played silly games,

We dreamed of what we would be when we grew up,

We did grow up and moved away,

Yesterday turned into years,

Years turned into decades,

I wonder, where is my friend ?

Yesterday I lived in another land,

Knew different people,

Had youth at my command,

My parents were alive then,

Yesterday disappeared,

I know not how, or when.

Today emerged,

I wonder, does anyone know where yesterday goes?

POETICALLY SPEAKING

Now write your own Yesterday poem:

Yesterday I

Yesterday

I wonder

I Know Who I Am

I am a human being,

Needing love and security,

I give them out and they come back to me.

I am a fighter,

I don't give up when troubles come

For they make me to be strong.

I am courageous,

I am not afraid of the unknown,

I'm equipped to face challenges head-on.

I am a winner,

It doesn't matter how many times I lose,

As long as quitting I do not choose.

I continue to play the game,

Until winning becomes my name.

I know who I am,

It doesn't matter what the critics say,

I attract good things my way.

I won't settle for second best

Or let others cause me to digress.

I know who I am.

POETICALLY SPEAKING

Follow the template below to write your own I **Know Who I Am** poem. Think big and dream big and dare to be anything you want to be. Never let anyone tell you that you cannot achieve your dreams. Live to prove them wrong.

I Know Who I Am

I am

I am

I am

I am

I Know who I Am

I Know Who I Am

About The Author

Georgette Lee was born and raised on the island of Barbados in the Eastern Caribbean. She was introduced to poetry as an elementary school student at Westbury Primary School, where she later worked as a teacher. She remembers vividly the joy her seven-year old students encountered writing Haiku poems. Mrs. Lee has taught at the high school and college levels in Nassau, Bahamas, and in Illinois, always spreading her love of and passion for poetry to her students. She is the author of a collection of personal poems, Seasons. She currently lives in Steger, Illinois with her husband, Charles, where she is pursuing doctoral studies in Special Education at the University of Illinois at Chicago.

Made in the USA